UTILITY

SPACE

Atlas of maladies
∾ Ventral side ∾

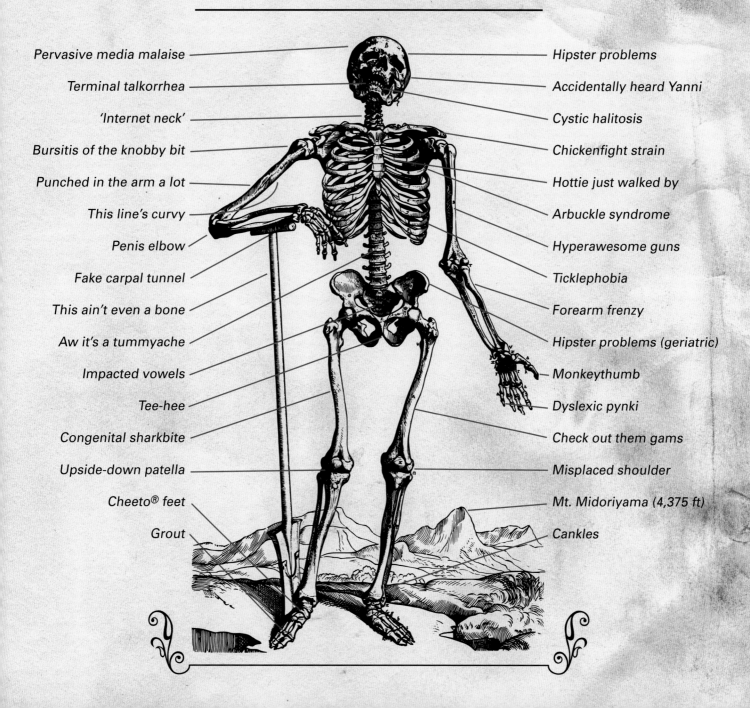

Pervasive media malaise

Terminal talkorrhea

'Internet neck'

Bursitis of the knobby bit

Punched in the arm a lot

This line's curvy

Penis elbow

Fake carpal tunnel

This ain't even a bone

Aw it's a tummyache

Impacted vowels

Tee-hee

Congenital sharkbite

Upside-down patella

Cheeto® feet

Grout

Hipster problems

Accidentally heard Yanni

Cystic halitosis

Chickenfight strain

Hottie just walked by

Arbuckle syndrome

Hyperawesome guns

Ticklephobia

Forearm frenzy

Hipster problems (geriatric)

Monkeythumb

Dyslexic pynki

Check out them gams

Misplaced shoulder

Mt. Midoriyama (4,375 ft)

Cankles

Atlas of maladies
∽ Dorsal side ∽

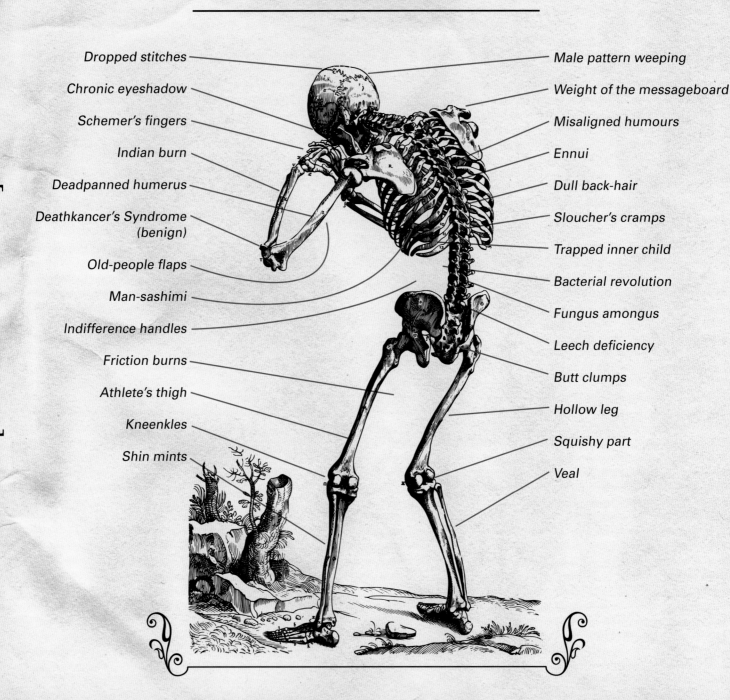

Douse all extremities vigorously with

Dropped stitches

Chronic eyeshadow

Schemer's fingers

Indian burn

Deadpanned humerus

Deathkancer's Syndrome (benign)

Old-people flaps

Man-sashimi

Indifference handles

Friction burns

Athlete's thigh

Kneenkles

Shin mints

Male pattern weeping

Weight of the messageboard

Misaligned humours

Ennui

Dull back-hair

Sloucher's cramps

Trapped inner child

Bacterial revolution

Fungus amongus

Leech deficiency

Butt clumps

Hollow leg

Squishy part

Veal

Clever Tricks to Stave off Death

by David Malki !

Member of the Guild of Valiant Efforts
South-west chapter

Wondermark Enterprises ∾
Los Angeles;
California U.S.A.

Dark Horse Books ∾
Milwaukie;
Oregon U.S.A.

Submerge lower body in

PUBLISHER ~ Mike Richardson

ART DIRECTOR ~ Lia Ribacchi

DESIGNERS ~ David Malki !, Cary Grazzini, and Heidi Whitcomb

ASSISTANT EDITOR ~ Katie Moody

EDITOR ~ Dave Land

UTILITY CORPSE ~ Justin Pierce

WONDERMARK:
CLEVER TRICKS TO STAVE OFF DEATH™

Published by **DARK HORSE BOOKS**
A division of **DARK HORSE COMICS, INC**
10956 SE MAIN STREET
MILWAUKIE OR 97222

darkhorse.com
wondermark.com

FIRST EDITION May 2009

ISBN-13: 978-1-59582-329-8

10 9 8 7 6 5 4 3 2 1
Printed in China

Mike Richardson, President and Publisher • Neil Hankerson, Executive Vice President • Tom Weddle, Chief Financial Officer • Randy Stradley, Vice President of Publishing • Michael Martens, Vice President of Business Development • Anita Nelson, Vice President of Marketing, Sales, and Licensing • David Scroggy, Vice President of Product Development • Dale LaFountain, Vice President of Information Technology • Darlene Vogel, Director of Purchasing • Ken Lizzi, General Counsel • Davey Estrada, Editorial Director • Scott Allie, Senior Managing Editor • Chris Warner, Senior Books Editor, Dark Horse Books • Rob Simpson, Senior Books Editor, M Press/DH Press • Diana Schutz, Executive Editor • Cary Grazzini, Director of Design and Production • Lia Ribacchi, Art Director • Cara Niece, Director of Scheduling

CONTENTS ~

Dr. VERNER'S HEALTH CORSET.

Sacrifice is Necessary to Mindlessly Follow Fashion :

Removes Health and Comfort of Body, along with Grace and Beauty of Form. **Three Garments in one.** Decried by all physicians. Price, by mail in London cord, $2.00; Satteen, $1.75. Once you wear, your Organs do not recover. Order Corset ten inches smaller than waist measure over the dress.

VERNER BROS., 351 Broadway, N.Y.

CORPULENCY

Speedily reduced by Tibbett's Hydriodic Obesity Pills, the only safe and infallible remedy for Obesity. No dieting or other inconvenience. Particulars, sealed, 2c. GEO. BURWELL, Chemist.

SKINNY WOMEN

Using "Adiposia" gain **10 lbs. per month.** Only genuine Fattening Preparation ever discovered.

A harmless and delicious Beverage which acts like magic. Particulars 4 cents.

GEO. BURWELL, Chemist.

OPIUM

Morphine Habit Cured in 10 days. We steal your stash. DR.J.STEPHENS, Lebanon, Oh.

MORPHINE AND OPIUM HABIT

Encouraged FREE. See what the commotion's about. 89 N. 5th, Lafayette,Ind.

CLARK'S REPLACEMENT TOES.

This False Toe is unrivaled for durability, simplicity, and cheapness. Adapted for Perambulation, Load-Bearing, middling Balance, and all purposes for which Toes are used. Circular and Price List free.

WM. P. CLARK. Wheeler, Pa.

Will Do It. Our Beard Elixir will force a **Mustache in 20 days. Full Beard** in 30. Sample package, postpaid, 15c.; one dozen, 75 cents. Agents wanted, mustache req'd. WESSON MFG., 5 E St., Providence, R.I.

NUT TAPPING MACHINE.

DURRELL'S PATENT.

Best Device for tapping nuts. When your Nuts need tapping, ***why turn to any but the best.*** Our Nut-Tappers are used in every industry or simply for recreation. Acknowledged to be an indispensable tool. No returns ; you know what you're getting. Manufactured by

HOWARD BROS., Fredonia, N. Y.

HOW CAN I OBTAIN A BEAUTIFUL COMPLEXION?

CAN wrinkles be removed permanently?
CAN pimples, blackheads, puffiness and coloration under the eyes be made to disappear?
CAN hollow, sunken cheeks be made plump?

NO, such so-called 'fixes' touted by this and other publications are totally impossible. You must learn to live with the problems your skin faces as you inevitably age. Send for booklets on coming to grips with reality. **I Used To Be So Beautiful, $1.50 ; I Cry All The Time, 25 cts.; Jealous of High-Schoolers, 50 cts.; Please God What's Wrong With Me Oh I Just Want To Be Happy But I Married The Wrong Man, 25 cts.** Treatise on saggy skin and bad complexion free. Mention this paper.

CHURCH OF WRINKOLOGY., Rochester, N.Y.

ON 30 DAYS' TRIAL

THIS NEW ELASTIC TRUSS

EGGLESTON'S
TRUSS

Has a Pad different from all others, is cup shape, with Self-adjusting Ball in center, adapts itself to all positions of the body, while the ball in the cup presses back the intestines, just as a person does with the finger. With light pressure, the Hernia is held securely day and night, and a radical cure certain. It is easy, disgusting and cheap. Sent by mail. Circulars free. **EGGLESTON TRUSS CO., Chicago, Ill.**

ELECTRICITY CURES

Deafness, Rheumatism, Paralysis, Heart Disease, Dyspepsia, Constipation, Spinal Diseases, Sick Headache, Gripp, Kidney, Liver Trouble, and all Chronic and Nervous Diseases, when applied by **Dr. Geo.F Webb's Jumper-Cables attached to a Car-Battery.** It has cured others, why not you. Testimonials and circulars **Free.** 10c. for our 100 page Disclaimer of Legal Liability. Address,

B. B. BLISS. U. S. Drawer No. 786, Iowa Falls, Ia.

FAT

FOLKS reduced, 15 lbs. a month. Miss M. Umphrey, Tekamah, Neb., says, "I lost 50 lbs. and feel splendid." No starving ; no sickness ; simply carve off excess flesh with razor. Particulars (sealed) 2c. HALL & Co., Box 404 V, St. Louis, Mo.

EYE SIGHT CAN BE RESTORED.

Cataracts, Scars or Films *Absorbed.* "Only Cost : Your Immortal Soul." Paralyzed Nerves RESTORED ; Diseased Eyes or Lids CURED. Glasses often discarded. Our Pamphlet giving HOME Treatment *free.* "SATAN," Glens Falls, N.Y.

MADAM ROWLEY'S ACID MASK (OR FACE GLOVE)

Trade Mark Registered.

To be Worn Three Times in the Week.

Is a natural scarifier for bleaching and disrupting the skin and creating complexional imperfections with acid.

It is **soft** and **flexible** in form, and can be easily applied and **worn** without **discomfort** or **inconvenience.**

It is recommended by **eminent physicians** and **scientists as a substitute for repeated surgery, with similar end effects.**

COSMETIC SURGERY may be fashionable, but endless treatments to repair the ravages of age can drain any purse. The Acid Mask applies **metered amounts of corrosive chemicals** to the face at **physician-dictated intervals** to **simulate the harmful effects of repeated surgery** at a fraction of the cost. *Your scars are indiscernible from those caused by surgical procedures costing thousands more.*

Illustrated Treatise, with full particulars, mailed free. Address, and kindly mention this magazine,

THE ACID MASK CO.,
1164 Broadway, New York.

COLUMBIA Dangerous Bicycles.

All ills solved by getting out-side, exercising in the fresh air, and tumbling to your doom. Resultant injury will put initial malady fresh out of mind. Thousands in daily use by doctors, lawyers, ministers, editors, merchants, etc., etc. No better way to shut up nosy neighbor—jaw-bone is easily broken by a fall from this device. Send 3c. stamp for catalogue to

COLUMBIA M'F'G CO., 18 Huntington Steet, Boston, Mass.

For Pleasure or Profit.

THE HOME SURGERY-THEATRE !

MAGIC LANTERNS,

and Stereopticons, OIL, LIME, OR ELECTRIC LIGHT, made by us, are *simply perfect* for PUBLIC or PRIVATE use. Comes with full kit of slides illustrating HORRID WOUNDS AND INFECTIONS so you can hold your first Exhibition on Day 1. Mention this publication.

J.B. Colt & Co. 16 Beekman St., NEW YORK. 189 La Salle St., CHICAGO, ILL.

---

if afflicted with sore balls, use Dr. THOMPSON'S BALL WATER

The above messages are placed by Sponsorship and are not recommended or endorsed—in fact, are heartily disclaimed—by the Publishers

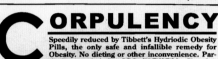

ABOUT THIS VOLUME

Its purpose

This manual contains comprehensive solutions to Life's many maladies. It is only through the fervent and repeated application of techniques such as the ones included that one may slow the onset of the inevitable.* No matter your major malfunction, you are invited to find its remedy in the pages to follow.

Using the manual

Each Section of the guide contains a different type of treatment. It is believed that this is the first time such a diversity of remedies, applicable to all persons regardless of condition,* has been made available to the public.

It is assumed that the reader has already arrived at a diagnosis of his or her condition prior to consulting this volume. Should this not be the case, **Section I**'s ATLAS OF MALADIES may be of use—but for a more comprehensive diaganosis the reader should consult our companion volume, *What's Killing You Today? An Index.*

Section II works in tandem with **Section III**, which presents a large number of comic-strips. This is ideal treatment for conditions in which the patient chiefly needs to be distracted from their pain for a while. *Examples: Leukemia; Mopiness*

The unfinished comic-strips in **Section IV** act as a reminder to the patient that everybody screws up once in a while, and not to be too hard on one's self. *This is ideal for conditions such as: Self-loathing; Perfectionism*

Section V is a TRUE STORY FROM HISTORY, recounted here to inspire the spirit and spur the patient on to glorious achievements in like fashion. *This treatment is recommended for: Aimlessness; Anemia; Black Bile, et cetera*

Finally, **Section VI** addresses more serious matters. Our flag-ship product, the trademarked MALADY MATRIX, is a new method of pairing a number of common conditions with frightfully simple solutions—for the first time in a volume weighing under fifteen Imperial pounds. Full directions begin on page 90.

Our promise

To be honest, at this point we've learned it's advisable, from a legal standpoint, to promise nothing. How about this: If the book poisons your dog, we will apologize. But beyond that, you're on your own.

---

*This claim has not been verified by an independent authority. Audit of records pending.

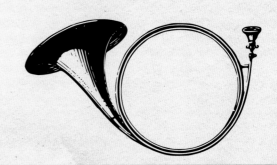

TOPICAL REFERENCE EXPLANATORY INDEX

As you peruse this volume, you may find that comic-strips originally published some time ago have lost their cultural context when collected here, and thus may appear puzzling or nonsensical. To avoid this confusion and afford the reader maximal enjoyment from even the most stale and rancid of comic-strips, we have provided the following index of background information.

Using the index

The symbol in the upper right of the page is used throughout the book to flag comics with potentially troublesome context issues. A number in the center of the symbol corresponds to the list at the right. Thusly may all comics in this collection be read without fear of bafflement.

Should you, despite the best efforts of this index, indeed experience disorientation, nausea, vertigo or tingling extremities upon reading an out-of-context comic, please refer to page 90 for instructions on how one may relieve these and many other symptoms endemic to the modern age.

1 You used to be able to bring liquids onto airlines
2 Pirates and ninjas were popular before overuse
3 The election included a number of minor issues
4 This movie engulfed all known media for a time
5 For a few years Ohio experienced this syndrome
6 At the time this was illegal for dogs but not men
7 Fighting 'house-to-house' was seen as ineffective
8 This was a common phrase among Armenians
9 Most doctors will not prescribe such a thing
10 James Brown is a deceased American entertainer
11 My birthday was not declared a holiday until 2007
12 At the time nobody had ever heard of Sarah Palin
13 In retrospect this proved ill-conceived and deadly
14 "Monkeypox" was a thing for a while
15 You can replace the first panel with anything you like; the effect is the same
16 Heavy use of this substance led to earlobe cancer
17 Rudolf Diesel was the inventor of the diesel engine
18 This was #1 on Google for "bin Laden sex tape"
19 It is things like this that make me feel very old
20 The media really banalized this horrible tragedy
21 The actual billboards at the time, of course
22 To be honest this joke is translated from Finnish
23 This did not used to be a legitimate concern
24 It was literally all anybody could talk about for weeks and weeks and weeks and weeks . . .
25 . . . until it came out and then everyone moved on
26 'Poison' the band was not popular even when this comic was written
27 A woman in New York did exactly this, all of it
28 There is no way to remove that amount of blood

dude do you think it will explode when I shoot it because that would be AWESOME

doesn't really matter whether 'read' is past tense or present tense

Breathe steam from placing in vaporizer

In which Roger attempts a Scheme

In which an Infant is quantified

'it exhibits a striking lack of comprehension of even the most rudimentary precepts of fire safety'

In which Life is freaking hard

because, you know, if you're, um, serious, I have some websites you can look at

In which Reality factors

also, webcomics

In which is marked an Anniversary of Birth

In which Melon provokes Mayhem

as your attorney i must advise you to in the future obtain signed releases prior to any further episodes of forkery

The Mayhem is compounded

and so they are

hey where did this muffin basket come from

NOTES THUS FAR

In which Aid comes to Marriage

140 horsepower, steam powered, 85 decibels idling—like all the best marital aids

In which Peter reveals Much

i am also self-employed

um, i guess you can keep the stuff addressed to 'resident'? because technically you would be the, uh, the only, like, resident

In which Education is Vital

the communist pirates are for the liberal arts subjects and there are erudite dinosaurs for computer science

kids if you are ever in this situation be sure to get a copy of the video

In which Blood is sucked

seriously what are you talking about

In which Marcie melts

WONDERMARK BY DAVID MALKI !
emote at WONDERMARK.COM
I'M MMMELLLLLTIIIINNNNNGGGGGG...
ARE YOU THROUGH BEING DRAMATIC
©2006 MALKI!

seriously

Participants in Democracy

WONDERMARK BY DAVID MALKI !
your civic duty is at WONDERMARK.COM
OKAY, C'MON, SAMPLE BALLOT PAGE EIGHT: PROPOSITIONS.
SHALL THE STATE CHARTER BE AMENDED AND ORDINANCE ADOPTED TO FUND A BOND MEASURE ALLOCATED FOR INFRASTRUCTURAL REPAIRS?
FISCAL IMPACT: STATE COSTS OF $8 BILLION OVER FIVE YEARS.
ARE YOU GETTING THIS?!
...OH, JULES, THERE'S JUST SO MUCH FOR YOU TO REMEMBER!
AND WE HAVEN'T EVEN LOOKED AT JUSTICE APPOINTMENTS.
KATIE, HONEY, YOU'RE BEING VERY SILLY. JULES IS A TURTLE.
THE POLLS CLOSE IN AN HOUR. AT A DEAD SPRINT HE'D BARELY MAKE IT TO THE KITCHEN.
©2006 MALKI!

jules moves slowly is the thing

In which Knowledge is Free

i have long held that this would totally work

In which a Houseguest factors

gasp! continuity!

NOOO BRAAAAAKESSS

ANOTHER TOUR-DE-FORCE BY NORBERT

That Norbert the Elephant remains one of the leading figures on the international dramatic stage is an indisputable fact of the world of theatre. His latest, *In which Misfortune is heralded,* is as pure and healthful a story as we have ever seen; simple for the most part, in no sense artificial, and wholly unmarred by straining for effect.

Mr. the Elephant's talents as an actor have never been questioned; his characters are never weak or vapid; the plots he finds himself embroiled in never commonplace; his incidents never tame. And in consecrating his craft to this noblest of uses, to the delineation of characters that are not a mere enigma, but an inspiration, he has solidified for himself a legacy as not only a member of the first rank of pachydermite stagesmiths, but even of mammalian actors in general. May he be commended so long as his power is ever employed in the cause of truth, of simplicity, and of purity.

Mr. the Elephant's latest drama is a quiet tale of love and sin and sorrow; it deals mostly with very plain people, living plain lives, with only one scene that may be regarded as belonging to the sensational. The characteristic feature of the story is not in its charming sketches of Life's peccadilloes, nor in the well-conceived and well-drawn characters, no one of whom, however, lacks a definite individuality—but in its genuine and shining exuberance of spirit, which in isolated moments suggests rather than deduces the divine lessons that even the commonest life has to teach us, if we are but apt pupils.

Dunk head in bucket filled with

In which Love is valued

then, with a mighty caw, the beast whirled and dumped a gallon of chalky white right on rosa's bonnet

In which Jody burns some Trash

but if you think it smells good now you should come back this afternoon when i add the hickory sauce

Create a dioama of your feelings using

Girls are Many-Splendored Things

five finger discount more like huge cardboard box discount

In which Mike flails around for a while

In which Libs are enmaddened

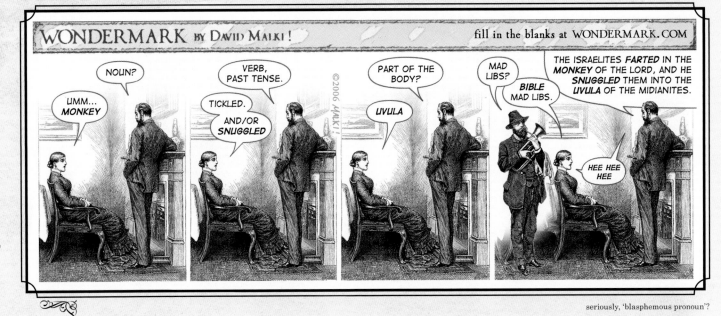

seriously, 'blasphemous pronoun'?

Snort

In which Babies become banal

there are no prizes for being a decent person. there are, however, several for eating cakes of butter, or choking down an imperial quart of milk in 3.2 seconds (1978 record)

WONDERMARK BY DAVID MALKI !
go for it at WONDERMARK.COM
FORGET THIS BORING LIFESTYLE! LET'S GO DO SOMETHING CRAZY!
LET'S WALK ACROSS THE COUNTRY!
YOU'RE INSANE.
IT'S THE MIDDLE OF SUMMER. WE WOULD DIE. ALONE, IN THE DESERT.
YOU ARE ALWAYS SUCH A POOP.
EXCUSE ME FOR WANTING TO STAY ALIVE.
©07 MALKI!
YOU SIT HERE EVERY DAY, WITH YOUR XBOX AND YOUR INTERNET AND YOUR NEVER-ENDING NETFLIX QUEUE.
APPARENTLY THAT'S ENOUGH FOR YOU.
BUT GUESS WHAT? I WANT SOMETHING MORE.
SO PUT THE BOOK DOWN, RANDY. WE'RE GONNA GO HAVE AN ADVENTURE.

Color by Marcus Thiele
themonkeymind.livejournal.com

wheeeee

Things to do before we DIE!!!!

Do IT

- Go to China (GREAT WALL) ~~(CHEAP DVDS)~~
- Mayan pyramids / Ziggurats
  → a.k.a. MEXICAN STAIRMASTER ←
- Finish novel
- Start novel
- Come up with idea for novel
- SCUBA DIVING
- NAT'L PARKS
- cheese shopping! IN BORNEO
- ~~Kite photography~~
- Tape record old people talking about WARS
- clean garage / house / LIFE
- cheese shopping! IN ECUADOR

In which our First President is baked

oh that hamilton what a prankster

In which James Brown is...well, you know

i worked on the television campaign for the movie 'robots' and at one point we used the james brown song 'dr. detroit' and there is a line that goes, 'get up offa that thang, dance 'til you feel better, get up offa that thang, tryn'ta relieve that pressure' and i swear it was so infectious i had to keep standing up and dancing feverishly before i could go on

In which a Plan ends poorly

through the quiet crackle of cooling embers she thought she almost heard him weeping. but it was probably just a faint hiss of steam, or else the wind, or else the sorrowful ghosts of her long year full of many purposeful misdeeds

In which Harvey is a Hater

sort of one of my 'things'

In which Alcoholism factors

now i remember

Core Beliefs called into question

Paint the lintels of your house with

daddy what's a phone book

A Moral Dilemma

note for international readers: hot topic is a store found in suburban shopping malls. they sell a bizarre combination of naughty novelties, goth gear like corsets and boots, and trendy logo shirts with 'clever' sayings or nintendo characters or the emblems of punk rock bands that were big a decade before the average customer was born. it is the dictionary definition of over-the-counter counterculture.

THE MOON, YOU SAY! ⌒

Ah, yes, the Moon! Of course! What? Yes! The Moon is one of my favorite subjects. Expert? Why, I wouldn't quite . . . Yes! Expert! Indeed. What would you like to know?

First off, it's important to define terms. By 'Moon' we are, of course, talking about a glowing round object that hangs in the night sky. Yes! *That* moon. All aboard? Onward!

The Moon has been around for ages. Ages and ages! Ancient Man looked upon the same moon that we do today. Well, at least a similar moon. What? Yes, it's surely the same! The Moon is forever and unchanging, unless something happens to it. What? Oh, *anything!*

Today's sciencemen know absolutely *loads* about the Moon. Some theorize that the Moon is made of cornmeal, balled up with lard and biscuit-wax and rolled across the heavens until it's smooth as a strongman's belly. It's hard to disprove anything in Science! Others think the Moon is a complicated optical reflection of the Sun, which is *also* in the sky unless it's cloudy, or night. But then that's when we see the Moon! So you see, options.

What? Two more paragraphs? Er. The Moon has perplexed thinkers for millennia, because no one has ever been able to satisfactorily answer the question: *what killed off the werewolves?* This phenomena likely involved the Moon. Also, *menses!* That is a woman thing that is carefully tied to the Moon, I believe with string. String is a key factor.

Tides! I nearly forgot to mention tides. The Moon stays so brilliant white because of Tide with Color-Fast Bleach. In conclusion, the Moon is a valuable resource that all of humanity must continue to be careful stewards of.

Mr. Swanson has High Hopes

o.j. simpson swanson

In which Johann gets a Job

always lead high and negotiate down

she had a double coupon for my heart

In which Giddiness is annoying

i left the album right here on my desk so i could show everyone later—how in the world could it have gotten caught in the shredder

In which a Metaphorical Fence is straddled

always hung up on nihilism for the sake of nihilism and never wanting to snuggle

In which Faith is Renewed

anyone read the 'ask a mexican' column in the alt-weeklies? true story—i went to college with that dude and
at one point apparently made him so mad that he wrote a letter to the school paper complaining about me

can you imagine? hours and hours and hours of sixteenth-notes

In which Shirley makes Dubious Claims to Insanity

but i wouldn't really call that 'weird'

In which That sounds like a Dare

In which Rick has Lofty Goals

Listen intently to the squishing sound made by

Color by Carly Monardo
www.carlymonardo.com

i just wanted someone to NOTICE me

MILESTONES IN CAR-ALARM HISTORY

Listen! I'm sorry if we *irritate* you, but we're an IMPORTANT PART OF HISTORY and I'm tired of us being so *marginalized!* Just *look* at some of the contributions car-alarms have made over the years:

1066 Warbler tries to warn Harold II of England of incoming arrow (unsuccessful, but a valiant effort)

1215 Selfless alarm chirps for 12 hours to frighten off birds which might have defecated on the Magna Carta

1368 Ming Dynasty named after the sound made by Zhu Yuanzhang's favorite alarm

1456 Gutenberg's Bible fitted with LoJack

1492 Columbus uses keyring remote to arm system on the *Santa Maria* from 70 yards away

1605 Car-alarm with a conscience rats out Guy Fawkes

1789 French peasants throw pebbles at Bastille warden's Honda; alarm distracts him from watching security monitors

1804 Napoleon crowns himself Emperor, crowns his car-alarm Co-Emperor

1865 Robert E. Lee surrenders to Ulysses S. Grant at Appomattox Auto Alarm & Stereo Installery

1903 After many failures, on December 17, Orville Wright, grumpy from losing sleep due to a loud car-alarm, tries *extra hard* to make the Wright Flyer fly

1945 83-hour marathon of ascending whoops from brave Mercedes-Benz drives Adolf Hitler to suicide

1969 Neil Armstrong & Edwin "Buzz" Aldrin greeted on the Moon with celebratory repetitive buzzers

1997 An alarm prevents a car from being stolen

In which Corporate Parentage is revealed

fresh squeezed at WONDERMARK.COM

works every time

In which Jamie feels Old

bones ache at WONDERMARK.COM

guys gender reassignment surgery is a very delicate subject for many people and i'll thank you not to trivialize it for a cheap gag okay SERIOUSLY :[

in fact i just noticed it on my way into town and wondered, 'hmm, what a bizarre pile of wrecked carriages and horse skeletons'

In which Patrick does a Double Take

The two men have had this conversation before.

maybe this is not the best time to mention that i honestly found your descriptions of my many heroic deeds both 1) a little over the top with the magic and 2) cribbed entirely from a harry potter book

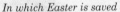

In which Easter is saved

hope you like chocolate!

In which Everyone is a Failure

In which Lamont suffers a Scare

still it's better to be safe right

In which Disappointment looms

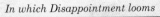

SO not in the mood

WONDERMARK by David Malki !

bright wide world at WONDERMARK.COM

Color by Carly Monardo
www.carlymonardo.com

in fact I married her largely BECAUSE she has never listened to 96.9 HITZ-FM

Play along at home

It's the fun game craze that's sweeping the charts! The . . . *game* charts. They have those, right? Game charts? Okay here we go—answers are upside-down at the bottom of the page in *traditional answer fashion.*

1 Now that it's rains white more than ever that one has the I still that you can be set under my umbrella

2 I observe you the person mirror, request, in order to change that method, in order to arrive on it

3 The terrestrial hand of my dream which takes the night when it integrates the light/write comes

4 Cheerful the himself of world gentleman appears with the land wage the trial that it takes

5 Make in order to grip me, make, to fall in love with likably persona, day of the week of 8 roads in me.

6 Same I want pistons and I cannot find them that other siblings cannot refuse great this, if a girl goes all inside the dimension and a round thing with itty bitty to your ace you derived from maintenance

7 Number the ape such as Fritos number the ape as a very simple man of the ape of the code of the rope of the feather/spring, and of the mountain with the smeared secret heart it warms on large: Number the ape as you

8 Whether you think, that I how would like to know a certain thing, the star where it comes out and there is no eye and comes out and is not the eye and is small

9 My cat is made to eat and, method, therefore the foreigner who is a possibility there of testing my weapon that has pleasure! where

Answers: 1—Rihanna, *Umbrella;* 2—Michael Jackson, *Man in the Mirror;* 3—Metallica, *Enter Sandman;* 4—Joy to the World; 5—Beatles, *Eight Days a Week;* 6—Sir Mix-A-Lot; *Baby Got Back;* 7—Jonathan Coulton, *Code Monkey;* 8—*Twinkle Twinkle Little Star;* 9—How Much Does a Shumway, from my unreleased 2001 rap album We So Pimp

also, smelly people

In which Tragedy strikes

also, vampire erotica

WONDERMARK BY DAVID MALKI !
yearn at WONDERMARK.COM
I CAN'T BEAR TO LIVE LIKE THIS ONE SECOND LONGER!
FORGET MY FATHER. FORGET THE LAWS OF MY KINGDOM.
IT'S JUST SO TERRIBLE, NOT BEING ABLE TO BE WITH YOU!
YEAH, WHATTA SHAME.
I WANT TO DO IT. I WANT TO LEAVE THE WATER AND BECOME ONE WITH MANKIND OF THE LAND.
MAYBE WE SHOULD RETHINK THIS PLAN.
MAYBE YOU SHOULD GROW SOME FRIKKIN LEGS
©07 MALKI !

and, you know...PEOPLE parts

In which Gerald faces Reality

WONDERMARK BY DAVID MALKI !
deal with it at WONDERMARK.COM
NOT GONNA BUY ANTHING, THEN, HUH?
THAT'S ALL RIGHT. I'M USED TO IT – CAN'T DO ANYTHING RIGHT THESE DAYS.
I'M JUST NOT GOOD AT THIS – NOT CUT OUT FOR THE LIFE.
SORRY TO BOTHER YA.
OH, GROW UP.
HUH?
SERIOUSLY, STOP WHINING. YOU'RE DOING FINE. DON'T YOU THINK EVERYONE ELSE HAS THE SAME INSECURITIES?
NOBODY'S EVER SATISFIED WITH THEIR OWN WORK. NOBODY MATURE, ANYWAY.
YOU'RE NOT SOME FREAKISH ABERRATION, YOU'RE JUST NORMAL.
IS THAT SUPPOSED TO BE COMFORTING?
©07 MALKI !

tell me, how exactly am I supposed to answer that without making you cry?

In which there are no Tracks

now we will never see the pandas humping :(

In which Something Happens

huh! I guess I never got around to checking the train schedule before embarking on this ridiculous excursion!

i would think it would be obvious from the way i always leave the dvd paused on that scene while we do it

i guess this would explain my increased tendency to shout at the television

In which Wendy learns Too Much

ever step onto the subway on a hot day and get just smacked in the face with a wave of b.o.? ewwwww

In which an Argument is formulated

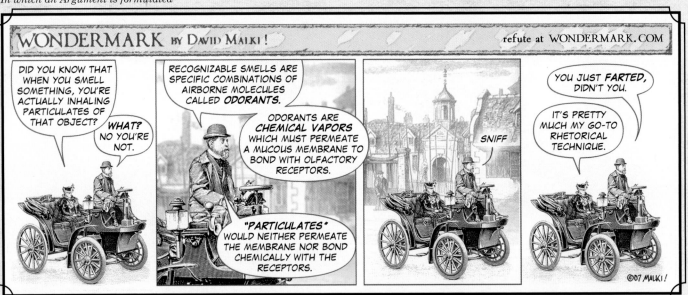

really, spoilsport, it is much funnier if you think you are breathing poop. and normally 'particulates' seals the deal.

Color by Alyssa Stock
www.rustydoves.com

'the most comprehensive encyclopedia ever will surely need six different close-ups from various angles'

Is this Comic Really Accurate?

When I first saw this comic I thought it was a gross distortion, but maybe it gets to some deeper truth that'll help the n00bs understand why we do things a certain way. But there are definitely things that could be cleaned up. Worth the trouble? BurritoFan75 15:59, 17 April 2007 (UTC)

Something like the NYT obviously meets Wikipedia:Reliable sources but this comic doesn't make the distinction that other print sources might not. Troublewithvampires 18:01, 17 April 2007 (UTC)

If you think it needs edits, DO IT instead of yapping away =P MushroomKing 09:14, 18 April 2007 (UTC)

Well I want to see if there's some kind of consensus so it's not all reverted 10 seconds later, you know? BurritoFan75 09:31, 18 April 2007 (UTC)

Why would your edits be reverted if you're adhering to Wiki guidelines? You said yourself there are things that could be cleaned up, so stop whinging and clean them up per Wikipedia:Be bold. PROBATOR 19:59, 18 April 2007 (UTC)

I hardly think working for consensus is 'whinging.' BurritoFan75 20:10, 18 April 2007 (UTC)

my balls are notable per Wikipedia:My balls lesboules 23:39, 18 April 2007 (UTC)

I don't think this comic has anything encyclopedic to say about Wikipedia or some battle that may or may not have happened. WP:AfD per Wikipedia:Notability. Sir 10 Lee 12:31, 4 June 2007 (UTC)

IS THE GENITALS THING REAL BECAUSE I GOT TO GET BUSY -- Preceding unsigned comment added by 43.134.305.821 (talk) 22:45 21 March 2008 (UTC)

In which Jed is asked an Impertinent Question

actually, birchwood, but that sure shut 'em up

In which Fruit goes Un-Sold

let me tell you all about this crazy dream i had—hey why is everyone leaving the room

In which Paul asks a Question of an Eel

basically i am looking for someone who thinks it is perfectly acceptable to eat an entire 5 lb bag of marshmallows in 13 minutes

In which This is Awesome

WONDERMARK BY DAVID MALKI !
i said check it at WONDERMARK.COM
AW, YEAH. CHECK THIS ACTION OUT.
VOOP
NYEARP
VOOP
NYEARP
VOOP
NYEARP
I'M NOT WEARING ANY UNDERWEAR.
YO I KNEW THIS WOULD GET YOU EXCITED
©07 MALKI !

i can tell by the tenting

little kernel buried in there shaking his tiny fist just yelling 'hogaaaaan'

The Scourge of Northern Europe

it's not like you haven't thought of it

then i drank thirty mountain dews and ran in circles around my couch for six hours

In which an Officer exercises Vigilance

but seriously let's have a look then

raw snake meat

WONDERMARK BY DAVID MALKI !

carefully consider at WONDERMARK.COM

SHREK THE THIRD OUTDOOR ADVERTISING CREATIVE MEETING

AND ON ONE BILLBOARD WE'LL SHOW ALL THE PRINCESSES, WITH THE TAGLINE 'GIRLS GONE MEDIEVAL'!

HA HA HA

I DON'T KNOW, IT SEEMS TO ME THAT ANY PUN ON OR PERMUTATION OF THE 'GIRLS GONE WILD' CONCEPT WOULD JUST INHERENTLY BE IN POOR TASTE, ESPECIALLY IN MARKETING DIRECTED AT CHILDREN.

ALSO, IT SENDS THE TACIT MESSAGE THAT 'GIRLS GONE WILD' IS A NORMAL AND ACCEPTABLE PART OF THE CULTURE – WHEN IN FACT IT'S SEEDY TRASH THAT THRIVES ON THE MOST CRASS AND DEBASED ELEMENTS OF HUMAN NATURE.

BESIDES, C'MON GUYS – WE CAN COME UP WITH SOMETHING FUNNIER.

INTERESTING PERSPECTIVE. JACK?

IT'S 'EDGY'.

SOLD

©07 MALKI !

Color by Carly Monardo
www.carlymonardo.com

21

guessing it went pretty much like this in real life, except with the wordy objection replaced by celebratory back-slapping

CREATIVE MEETING!

C'mon, everyone into my office. Squeeze on those couches. Did everyone watch the feature? First thoughts? I don't care if you *liked* it, New Guy, we're talking about *marketing*. Any kind of slasher film is always going to be a hard sell for moms, so we need to play up the 'family' aspect during a daytime campaign, spots on *The View* and so on. Play down the moral repugnance as much as we can. Are there any jokes we can carve out? As you pull your selects, watch for lines we can Franken into some attitude. Attitude, edgy but not scary, friendly-spooky family fun. Okay? I want to see scripts in the morning. We're up against three other houses so let's get cracking. Make it special!

MEET THE TAYLORS.

THEY LOVE SPENDING TIME WITH EACH OTHER

AND NOTHING COULD TEAR THEM APART.

BUT WHEN A SOCIOPATHIC GARBAGEMAN WITH A HYDRAULIC TRASH COMPACTOR MOVES IN NEXT DOOR

NOTHING WILL BE ABLE TO PRY THEM APART.

THIS HOLIDAY SEASON

ONE FAMILY

IS LEARNING THE TRUE MEANING OF TOGETHERNESS.

KEEP FINGERS CLEAR
RATED R

you know the old argument. 'I pay for the food my body uses to make this hair, and what, you expect me to just throw it away?!'

In which Kevin shops for Hats

hey what about that one with the fake fruit, THAT one has potential

In which a Scheme is hatched

excuse me, ma'am? after watching your behavior in the parking lot, i thought you might be interested in one of these 'crazy psycho offset cards'

In which Paul oils his Brakes

trenton! don't forget to make an entry in your idiot log! we'll be going over the week's records once we get to nana's and it doesn't take much disappointment to topple the poor woman's carefully-balanced decades of regret

i.t. stands for intestinal torsion

if you get one of those cheap phones with the candy inside, you can have the freedom to speak your mind PLUS delicious candy

yeah. the discourse has been reduced to this.

The Failure of an Entrepreneur

the rock may shed light on questions raised by previous rocks j.k.r. may or may not have touched, and may also raise new questions to be addressed by future rocks

a marvelous soufflé

WONDERMARK by David Malki !

make it good at WONDERMARK.COM

Panel 1: AAAH! THAT WALT-WHITMAN-HEADED *BAT* IS BACK! / I TOLD YOU TO BE MORE *UPTIGHT* WITH YOUR GARDENING! YOU'RE INVITING IN ALL SORTS OF CRAZIES. / WHAT WITH YOUR *ASSORTED WILDFLOWERS.*

Panel 2: O LISTEN, UNIMPRESSED MORTALS – / SHALL I GRANT YOU EACH SOME WISH? / SOME SMALL BOON, SOME FAVOR, SOME EASY ACCESSORY AGAINST EACH DAY'S UNEASY BURDEN? / SO THAT YOUR YOUNG, HANDSOME FACES MAY SHINE WITH NEWFOUND DELIGHT?

Panel 3: A *WISH,* EH? WELL, LET'S SEE HERE... / WITH ONLY ONE SHOT, I BETTER MAKE IT GOOD... / WISHING FOR MORE WISHES IS ALWAYS OUT... / HOW ABOUT WISHING FOR THE BEST POSSIBLE WISH? WOULD THAT EVEN *WORK?*

Panel 4: OKAY, I GET IT, YOU WISH YOU WERE MORE DECISIVE. / HOW ABOUT YOU? / I WANT TO BE ABLE TO JUMP INTO MY PANTS WITH BOTH LEGS AT ONCE. / OH MAN YES! *AWESOME!* / IN FACT! *BAM!* NOW *EVERYONE* CAN DO THAT!

Color by Marcus Thiele
themonkeymind.livejournal.com

if only comics were real :(I guess I will have to settle for broken ankles

WHAT DID YOU ASK FOR FROM THE WALT-WHITMAN-HEADED-BAT?

"Oh, just a spot of Earl Grey to make it through the afternoon, and some biscuits for it to wet besides."
J.A. FRANZIBALD, PIERRE, S.D.

"I asked for a new washing machine, but didn't realize till later I could've asked for ever-clean clothes."
MARTINE T. PARSNIP, TORONTO, ONT.

"I left it to the beast—'entertain me!' I cried. 'In whatever fashion best suits my character!' In return, he farted."
MRS. H. WELLSLEY, BIRMINGHAM, G.B.

"He was flyin' all around and why, I couldn't think of nuthin cleverer than a first edition *Leaves of Grass.*"
BILL SNAGG, SPOKANE, WA.

"I said 'a bottomless bottle of Jack,' and that's what I got. A glass bottle with no bottom. Har-de-har-har."
FREAKISH DRUNKEN FROG, FLA.

"Six rolls of duct tape, 80 ft. of rope, and five overstuffed pillows."
DR. JAS. HUTTON, KINGSBURY, CONN.

"Mmmrrfffff."
NAME WITHHELD, KINGSBURY, CONN.

I want action at WONDERMARK.COM

WOW, WHAT A GREAT TURNOUT! I DIDN'T THINK THIS MANY PEOPLE WERE INTERESTED IN *POISON.*

ARE YOU *KIDDING?!* "EVERY ROSE" BASICALLY *DEFINED* A MARGINALIZED MINI-GENERATION. IT WAS LIKE MY *ANTHEM* SENIOR YEAR.

WAIT, ARE YOU TALKING ABOUT "POISON" THE *BAND?*

TOTALLY!

BRET MICHAELS BASICALLY *RAISED* ME. THROUGH THE TAPE PLAYER IN MY CAMARO.

OH! AND I'M PRETTY SURE THE LYRICS FOR "RIDE THE WIND" WERE AT LEAST *PARTIALLY* INSPIRED BY ONE OF MY FAN LETTERS.

IS *EVERYONE* HERE FOR POISON THE BAND?

UH, *YEAH,* HOMBRE! I'VE ALREADY MET UP WITH "RATTTRAP" FROM THE OLD LISTSERV.

WELL, I FEEL LIKE AN IDIOT NOW.

WHY, WHAT ARE *YOU* HERE FOR?

NOTHING. LISTEN, I'D *SKIP* THE PUNCH.

©07 MALKI!

(26)

n-no reason, it's just—uh, it's just GRAPE, and you do NOT look like a guy who appreciates that fakey grape flavor. I mean it would probably put you off your whole night. And this is YOUR night.

In which Mom gets to the Bottom of Things

one step ahead at WONDERMARK.COM

THERE'S THE LITTLE SCAMPS!

WHAT HAVE YOU KIDS BEEN UP TO TODAY?

NOTHING! NOTHING AT ALL! EVERYTHING'S *TOTALLY FINE!*

I UH DON'T THINK I'VE *EVER* BEEN IN THE GARAGE

WE HAVEN'T EVEN BEEN *IN* THE GARAGE! WE'VE JUST BEEN, UH, *UPSTAIRS!*

OH, DEAR.

DO I NEED TO GO LOOK IN THE GARAGE?

NO! NOT AT ALL!

I MEAN, NOT UNLESS YOU WANT TO SEE *CARS!* THE CARS ARE STILL IN THERE!

WE DIDN'T MOVE THEM! WHY WOULD WE HAVE MOVED THEM? WE *WOULDN'T'VE!*

YEAH I MEAN WE'RE JUST *KIDS*

©07 MALKI!

I *KNOW* WHAT YOU'RE DOING.

YOU'RE *PRETENDING* TO HAVE DONE SOMETHING WRONG, SO I'LL GO LOOK AND NOTHING WILL BE THE MATTER...

THAT WAY, I'LL EVENTUALLY GROW *TIRED* OF LOOKING EVERY TIME YOU KIDS ACT NERVOUS, THUS *FREEING* YOU TO CAUSE *ALL SORTS* OF MISCHIEF!

WOW.

WE *DID* IT. SHE'S *NUTS.*

AS LONG AS SHE DOESN'T LOOK IN THE GARAGE

once you grow up, you have to just sit around all day figuring out how your children are trying to deceive you. if you let your guard down even for a moment, all of a sudden they are seventeen years old breaking the lock on your toolshed and selling all your power tools for meth money.

In which Walt makes a Suggestion

WONDERMARK by David Malki !

dig deeper at WONDERMARK.COM

WE'RE STILL REPORTING ON THE TRAGIC CASE OF FORTY MINERS TRAPPED IN A CAVE-IN. WITH US *LIVE* IS MINE FOREMAN *EUSTACE PROWLYBUCKET.*

EUSTACE, WHAT'S THE SITUATION? ANY *PROGRESS* SINCE WE TALKED TO YOU LAST?

IN THE LAST *FOUR MINUTES?* NO, WALT, I CAN'T REALLY SAY SO.

SO WHAT'S YOUR NEXT MOVE?

WELL, RIGHT NOW I'M TRYING TO FIND SOMEONE TO TAKE OVER THESE *INTERVIEWS,* SO I CAN GET BACK TO WORK ON THE ACTUAL *MINE.*

NOW I'M NO *MINING EXPERT,* OF COURSE, BUT HERE IN THE STUDIO WE HAD A *THOUGHT...*

IS IT POSSIBLE THE MINERS ARE JUST *LOST?*

HAVE YOU TRIED *SHOUTING?*

©07 MALKI!

THWACK

In which She's Just Making Sure

WONDERMARK by David Malki !

sneak around at WONDERMARK.COM

OH, HENRY! THIS PICNIC WAS *JUST* WHAT I NEEDED. I GET SO *WORN OUT* HAVING TO WATCH EMILY ALL THE TIME.

SHE GETS INTO SUCH *MISCHIEF!*

SPEAKING OF WHICH – WHO'S LOOKING AFTER HER NOW?

AH, I'M SURE SHE'S *FINE.* PROBABLY DOING *GIRL STUFF* – PLAYING WITH DOLLS, YOU KNOW, OR BAKING *MUFFINS* OR SOME CRAP LIKE THAT.

WE CANNOT TELL *ANYBODY.*

©2006 MALKI!

cell phone lines were jammed. everyone was so busy fielding concerned calls from out-of-state relatives that they didn't notice the GIANT METEOR OH NOOOOOOOO

In which Sanders files a Claim

Color by Mario Martín
dimlightcreatures.wordpress.com

conversely, everyone quieter than you may actually be tolerable to be around

I CAN'T TAKE IT

That's it! I'm done! I can't take living next to Gary anymore. Every day it's the same old story, complaining about absolutely everything. To listen to him, you'd think he's some paragon of virtue we should all aspire to! Well, nuts to that. We're *fighting back*.

Gary's the president of our homeowners' association, so we can't just avoid him. But we can't *live* with him either! So me and the neighbors got a plan together. Jimbo's a great vocal impressionist, and Suzanne's handy with tools, so we're gonna make ourselves a Gary *robot* full of recordings. That way, we can kill the real deal however we want, set the robot up in his yard, and nobody will ever be the wiser! *Foolproof.*

STOP BOTHERING ME

Everyone nicer than me is a sap! Everyone meaner than me is a jerk! Everyone poorer than me is lazy! Everyone richer than me is corrupt! Everyone cleaner than me is obsessive! Everyone dirtier than me is slovenly! Everyone skinnier than me is a stick! Everyone fatter than me is a whale! Everyone *bzzzt--CCCHKK-TKK-VVVRRTT-T-T-T SSSSSSS GGKBVVVT-- ERROR----MEMORY FRAGMENTED----REINITIALIZING----EE- EEEEverrryone-CCCHTK *kk* Everyone bigger than me is a dog! Everyone underneath me is a part! Everyone has a done me is a fog! Everyone wonderful me is a name! Everyone is a man me is a rock! Everyone neoprene me for the lake! Everyone underfound meanism preek! STOP IT--STOP IT--STOP IT

In which All Needs are met

really? rump roast didn't go on the first day?

In which a Meeting goes poorly

i have come so close to doing this so many times

In which Sonya cannot be Idle

In which the Record is clear

YOU ARE NOT HELPING YOUR CASE HERE MARSHA

In which She's Just Making Sure

cell phone lines were jammed. everyone was so busy fielding concerned calls from out-of-state relatives that they didn't notice the GIANT METEOR OH NOOOOOOOO

Color by Kory Bingaman
www.korybingaman.com

AGAIN?!

How does HE rate a stalker?

I just don't understand it! I've done everything. I've left personal information un-shredded in garbage cans. I've posted my home address on MySpace. I've even dropped hints around town that I live alone and that my blinds are prone to malfunction. But I can't seem to attract a peeping Tom, much *less* a full-on, photo-leaving *stalker!*

I mean, come on! I'm young. Relatively attractive, let's be honest. I do a lot of interesting things during the day—I mean, a *good* stalker will be interested in the mundane stuff most of all, the stuff that affords him a window into my everyday life so that he can imagine himself participating in it. But I joined a gym, so I go outside in workout clothes a lot, and come back all sweaty; and sometimes I also do aerobic tapes in front of the living-room window. Stuff to really hook all the beginning stalkers and help them gradually assemble an idealized construct of me in their imaginations. I tie my garbage bags only loosely and leave the bin lids half-open. And I get *nothing!* Do you people need an *engraved invitiation?*

What really chaps is to see that Boy Scout three houses down get all the attention. I think his great-uncle's second wife used to be married to John Ashcroft or something, so the weirdos trickle down to him...but he does *nothing* to warrant it. I should know! I trailed him for a while, to see what he was doing that I could learn from, but he's always shyly ducking into and out of his car, keeping his drapes fully drawn, almost playing hard-to-get. Hmmm. Maybe *that's* the secret.

Marcus will use any excuse to get out of wearing pants.

In which Jasper takes One Bite Too Many

I'm looking forward to 2159 when they finally get the fake chocolate flavor into the realm of acceptable

BAD IDEA COMICS ❧

As therapeutic and informative as these comic-strips have been, it is sometimes helpful to know that others have occasional failings in life as well. On this and the following pages, please find examples of this phenomenon as documented by our forensic researchers.

These comics have been rescued from the scrap-bin against the fervent wishes of the author, in the hopes that the lessons of their failure will be particularly insightful.

FOLLOWING THAT ❧

Please find the long-form graphic story entitled "Ransom!", originally published in the *MySpace Dark Horse Presents* anthology in Spring 2008. The version of the story contained in this book has been revised somewhat since its initial publication, and is in many ways a SUPERIOR version to any previously seen in any milieu.

In which Hearty Chaps blather

In which Automated Spanking Privileges are abused

In which Perambulation meets Abomination

In which it All Comes Together

my subconscious has been making comics again

RANSOM!
A WONDERMARK TALE
by David Malki !
WELL, HELLO, MORNING. IT IS COLD AS BALLS OUT HERE.
WARREN. SHUSH.
WHAT? AM I NOT ALLOWED TO MENTION HOW NUT-FREEZINGLY FRIGID IT IS?
SOME NON-NUT-TALK STATUTE IN EFFECT ALL OF A SUDDEN? WHAT IS THIS, A POLICE STATE?
WE GOT RIGHTS. AND RIGHT NOW THEY'RE ALL CONTRACTED UP INTO OUR ABDOMENS NEXT TO OUR LEFTS, AM I RIGHT, FELLAS?
IT'S NOT APPROPRIATE CONVERSATION FOR THE PALACE GROUNDS.
THE ROYAL COURT IS STILL IN SHOCK FROM THE KIDNAPPING LAST NIGHT.
BESIDES, YOU SHOULD SHOW SOME RESPECT FOR THE DEAD. LET US BEAR OUR PALL WITH A GRIM, SPOOKY AIR OF SILENCE.
GRIM, GRIM. SPOOKY, SPOOKY.
WARREN.
I SWEAR THIS GUY MUST WEIGH FIVE HUNDRED POUNDS.
PROBABLY WHY HE JOINED THE KIDNAPPING RING.
– "MEETINGS ARE ON MONDAYS."
– "THERE'S REFRESHMENTS, RIGHT?"
"YEAH, WE TRADE OFF BRINGING DONUTS."
"COUNT ME IN! OH, WHAT'S YOUR RIDICULOUS CAUSE, AGAIN?"
"NOTHING. LOOK, HEY, WE GOTTA GO KIDNAP THE PRINCESS. YOU WILL MOST LIKELY DIE. THEN WE'LL HAVE DONUTS AFTERWARDS!"
FIE! WHILE THE PRINCESS BE IMPERILED, YE SHOULD KEEP YER TONGUE HELD FROM WALLYWAGGIN' SO!
LADY, I AM TEMPTED TO KILL YOU JUST FOR THE WARMTH OF YOUR ENTRAILS.

BIRD ON THE MOVE

SIR LAURENCE VON HAWKINGTON

STORY Continues.

HO THERE! CHOPPY SEAS, WHAT? HAVE YOU SEEN A ROWBOAT COME BY HERE LATELY?
MARK GET THE GUN GET THE GUN QUICK NO SUDDEN MOVES
I DIDN'T BRING THE GUN. I'M TIRED OF THESE OUTINGS ALWAYS BEING SO VIOLENT.
NO, RIGHT THERE IN THE GUITAR CASE! I REMEMER LOADING IT ABOARD!
AH!
THE BITTER WAFT OF RAILROAD OIL! THE TRAIL GROWS WARM ANON!
I TAKE MY LEAVE, CHAPPIES!
THAT WAS AN ACTUAL GUITAR. YOU KNOW, FOR THE LONELY HOURS.
ARRRGGHHH MARK I TOLD YOU I DO NOT WANT TO HEAR YOUR DEMO
IT'S COOL! IT'S COOL! JUST IF YOU COULD FORWARD MY MYSPACE TO YOUR FRIEND WHO WORKS IN A&R IS ALL!
GUYS I THINK WE MIGHT HAVE A PROBLEM
WHAT KIND OF PROBLEM?
THE LEGENDARY RAILROAD COVE!
SITE OF THAT INFAMOUS ZEPPELIN DISASTER!
O DARK DAY! WHEN LOCOMOTIVES FELL LIKE STEEL HAIL FROM THE HEAVENS...

AND THAT MUST BE THE LIGHTHOUSE WHERE OLD MAN McGINTY PLAYS HIS CURSED ACCORDION UNTIL THE END OF TIME!
WEARING HIS FINGERS TO THE BONE EACH NIGHT, ONLY TO SEE THEM HEALED EACH DAWN! WHAT TORTURE!
H-HOLY CRAP A TALKING BIRD
HOW THE SPIRITS HAUNT THIS BEDEVILED PLACE!
THE PSYCHIC ECHOES OF SOULS IN TORMENT INFUSE THE VERY ROCK! OH LORDY!
I – I THINK MY...
I THINK MY NIPPLES ARE TINGLING
WHICH OF COURSE IS WEIRD IN A LOT OF WAYS

STORY *Continues.*

AHA! A CABIN, OF SORTS! PERHAPS...A SHANTY?
THE RAMSHACKLE ABODE OF MY PREY, I PRAY!
HEE HEE PREY, PRAY... GOTTA WRITE THAT ONE DOWN
CAREFUL! MUSTN'T LET THE WATCH-BEAR SEE ME!
CAREFUL! MUSTN'T LET THE BIRD KNOW HE'S BEING FRIKKIN LOUD
WILTON FIFTH EARL OF BEARMOOR
YOU GUYS HEAR SOMETHIN'?
SOUNDS SORT OF LIKE THE WATCH-BEAR TEARIN' UP A BIRD.
...YUP, THAT'S FEATHER-RENDIN'. I'D KNOW IT ANYWHERE. WHAT WITH THE CHILDHOOD I HAD.
D'YA THINK IT WAS A SPY BIRD? YOU THINK THEY KNOW WHERE WE ARE?
I KNEW RAILROAD COVE WAS TOO SPOOKY A HIDEOUT FOR ME TO REALLY DEAL WITH MENTALLY
IT'S FINE. NO ONE KNOWS WE'RE OUT HERE. HOW COULD THEY?
I DON'T KNOW, MAN— YESTERDAY I FOUND A MENU FROM A THAI RESTAURANT ON THE DOORKNOB.
YEAH, BUT THOSE ARE LEFT BY GHOSTS. NOT BY PEOPLE.
Y-YOU'RE SO YOUNG TO BE INVOLVED WITH SUCH BRUTISH FOLK, AREN'T YOU?
YOU BETTER BE QUIET.
I'M SUPPOSED TO HONK IF YOU TRY TO USE RHETORIC ON ME.

OKAY. YES. OKAY. GOT IT.
THAT'S FINE. THAT'S A GOOD POINT.
THIS ISN'T THE TIME FOR CHIT-CHAT. THIS IS LIFE AND DEATH. THIS IS SURVIVAL.
A GOOD PERSON WOULD HELP ME. ARE YOU A GOOD PERSON, SWEETIE?
DO YOU HAVE ANY CANDY?
I — WELL, NO, NOT RIGHT AT THE MOMENT, NO. BUT I CAN —
HONK HONK HONK HONK HONK HONK HONK
SINGING TELEGRAM FOR THE KING!
I'LL TAKE IT. HIS MAJESTY IS INDISPOSED.
HOW YOU GONNA TAKE IT? IT'S A SINGING TELEGRAM.
ER — YOU CAN GIVE ME THE MESSAGE, AND I'LL PASS IT ALONG TO THE KING.
NAW, MAN, THAT AIN'T GONNA HAPPEN. THIS IS A SINGING TELEGRAM FOR THE KING, NOT FOR SOME PENCIL-NECK SNOOTY DUDE. NO OFFENSE.
WELL, UH...WHAT IF I WERE TO SING THE MESSAGE TO THE KING? WOULD THAT WORK?
IF IT'S UP TO ME? NO DOUBT. I'D LET YOU IN ON IT. ASSUMIN' YOU'VE GOT A GOOD ALTO.
BUT IF YOU SCREW IT UP, IT'S MY CHECK GETS DOCKED. SO NAW. I AIN'T GONNA TEACH IT TO YOU.
SIGH
VERY WELL. STRAIGHT ON, THEN. I'LL RING AHEAD.
TEEEEEELLLEGRAM
COMIN' THROUGH WITH A TEEEEELLLEGRAM FOR THE KIIIIIIINGGG
...AND SO I SAID, "SURE — IF YOU DON'T MIND BRAISED BEEF!"
HA HA HA HA HA
YO WASSAP Y'ALL I GOT A TELEGRAM HOMIES

STORY *Continues.*

THIS LOOKS LIKE THE ROOM WHERE THE KING MIGHT BE AT.
WHO DISTURBS THE KING SO? GUARDS! FEED THIS MAN INTO THE CHIPPER AT ONCE!
PLEASE, SIRE – IT MAY BE A MESSAGE FROM THE KIDNAPPERS! PERHAPS A RANSOM DEMAND?
I WILL GIVE YOU A HINT. THAT IS WHAT IT IS.
WELL? OUT WITH IT, THEN!
YOU'RE SURE YOU ARE ACTUALLY THE KING?
GUARDS!
OKAY HERE WE GO.
YO WE GOT THE HOMEGIRL AND I'LL LAY OUT WHAT WE'RE ASKIN'
NEED A FAT WAD O' BILLS / BEST NOT LOOK LIKE IT BEEN FASTIN'
Y'ALL MAKE WITH THE DOUGH FO' WE GIVE UP YOUR HO
NOW YOU KNOW TO MAKE IT FLOW TO THE FOLLOWING P.O.
...BOX
THAT WAS HORRIBLE.
STUDIO MIX HAS SOME PHAT SAMPLES. MP3 AVAILABLE ON MY WEBSITE.
MC MUTTONCHOPZ
MYSPACE.COM/ SIDEBURNS342
RINGADINGDING ON A PORCH SWING
GET INTO THE SWING OF THINGS
I'M STANDIN OUT THE FRONT LIKE
A LOBSTER MADE OF ONION RINGS
COME ON MAKE THE CALL YOU KNOW
YOU WANT A SINGING TELEGRAM
I GOTTA SCRAPE YER EARS OUT LIKE
A Q-TIP MADE OF CHRISTMAS HAM
SPITTIN CRAZY LYRICS LIKE
A LETTER FROM THE SON OF SAM
MAKIN OTHER SUCKERS LOOK LIKE
TURTLES IN A TRAFFIC JAM
BOYEEE

I CAN'T BELIEVE THE KING REFUSES TO PAY THE RANSOM!
SIR, WHY ARE YOU SURPRISED? ISN'T IT YOUR BELIEF THAT THE KING SHOULD NEVER NEGOTIATE WITH TERRORISTS?
I HOLD **LOTS** OF BELIEFS, MY BOY. **MANY** OF THEM CONTRADICTORY. IT'S WHAT'S GOTTEN ME TO THIS LEVEL OF GOVERNMENT.
BUT STILL... DOESN'T HE **LOVE** HIS EXCEEDINGLY BEAUTIFUL DAUGHTER?
OF COURSE YOU DO. **EVERYONE** DOES.
I KNOW **I** SURE DO!
DO **YOU,** LORD BONEHAT?
I **SAID**
EVERYONE DOES.
AND AFTER THE RANSOM IS **PAID** TO **MY ACCOMPLICES**...I SHALL **RUN AWAY** WITH HER!
AS **I** HAVE BEEN, ALL THESE YEARS, GAZING ON HER FROM **AFAR, DREAMING** OF THE DAY WHEN WE COULD BE TOGETHER!
I'M... I'M **DYING,** MY LORDSHIP
AGGKKKKK
NO, I MEAN LIKE **LEGITIMATELY DYING**
WELL, OF **COURSE.** NOW YOU KNOW MY PLAN. YOU CAN'T BE ALLOWED TO LIVE.
IN THAT CASE... **ARRGGHHHKKKKK...** REMEMBER TO PICK UP YOUR DRY CLEANING ON MONDAY
DO YOU HEAR SOMETHING? LIKE A – I DON'T KNOW, THIS SOUNDS DUMB, BUT LIKE A **SCREAM OF AGONY?**
I HEAR A MOUSE SCRATCHING AROUND IN THE WALL.
A **MOUSE.** YEAH, IT'S PROBABLY JUST A MOUSE.
NO, THAT WOULD – THAT WOULD BE **RIDICULOUS.**
IT'S DEFINITELY **NOT** LORD BONEHAT PLOTTING TREASON AND STRANGLING HIS HOUSEBOY.

STORY *Continues.*

JUST GOT WORD FROM LORD BONEHAT.
RANSOM'S ON ITS WAY. LOAD UP THE "PACKAGE" FOR TRANSPORT TO THE PALACE.
JUST GOT WORD? HOW IN THE WORLD DID YOU JUST GET WORD?
SINGING TELEGRAM.
AWW, I MISSED IT. WAS IT GOOD?
IT WAS NOT.
REALLY? THE ONLY WAY TO FULFILL THE PLAN IS SERIOUSLY TO GIVE ME A HERNIA?
HRRRGGHH
TO COMPLY WITH THE LAW, TECHNICALLY WE ARE SELLING THE KING A PIANO.
ANYTHING THAT HAPPENS TO BE INSIDE THE PIANO IS OUR GIFT TO HIM.
HEH HEH HEH

HEH HEH HEH

HEH HEH HEH

THE MAN WITH THE PIANO IN HIS ROWBOAT IS CHUCKLING QUIETLY TO HIMSELF.

DUDE, THAT'S NOTHING. THIS MORNING I SAW A BIRD DELIVER A MONOLOGUE.

...I'M NOT SURE *WHEN* LARRY WILL RETURN, ERNESTO. WHEN HIS TASK IS COMPLETE, I SUPPOSE.

THE PLUCKY LITTLE FELLOW IS NOTHING IF NOT *THOROUGH.*

LADY! *FORGET* TALKING TO HIM — HE'S CONVINCED THAT BIRDS ARE A CABAL OF ALIENS WHO SECRETLY CONTROL THE ECONOMY.

TO GET TO THE PALACE, FOLLOW THIS ROAD FOR HALF A MILE, THEN TURN LEFT AT THE HUNDRED-FOOT-TALL PILE OF FLOWERS AND HANDWRITTEN POEMS ABOUT THE PRINCESS.

THE ROAD TO THE PALACE IS *FECKLESSNESS* AND *RUDE BEHAVIOR!*

PARDON, IS THIS THE ROAD TO THE PALACE? I HAVE A DELIVERY.

IF YOU HIT THE *CANDLELIGHT VIGIL,* SLIT YOUR OWN WRISTS. YOU WON'T MAKE IT OUT OF THERE ALIVE.

SO...IS THAT THE INTERSECTION, OR...?

OH, *THANK YOU!* YOU SEE, I'M JUST DELIVERING THIS NOT-AT-ALL-SUSPICIOUS *PIANO* TO HIS MAJESTY.

DON'T NEED YOUR LIFE STORY. NOW YOU'RE BLOCKING THE ROAD.

STORY Continues.

camphor and cod-liver oil

WE'RE WAIIIITING!
YOU GOT FIRED, DIDN'T YOU? YOUR SINGING TELEGRAMS SUCKED.
NOW YOU'RE A DELIVERY GUY OR SOMETHING. ANYTHING YOU CAN DO TO GET CLOSE TO THE PALACE.
YOU SYCOPHANTS MAKE ME SICK. THE ROYAL FAMILY HAS ENOUGH TO DEAL WITH WITHOUT LEECHES LIKE YOU HANGING AROUND.
LISTEN TO YOU. JES' TALKIN'. DON'T CARE WHAT SPILLS OUT. THIS MAN COULD BE A PERFECTLY NICE PERSON.
THIS IS WHY YOU WERE PASSED UP FOR PROMOTION.
BONEHAT! THE PRINCESS IS RETURNED! STOP QUAKING AND STAMMERING WITH RELIEF!
LET US OPEN THE PIANO AND END HER LONG ORDEAL!
BUT – BUT – BUT – UM – UH – BUT – UM –
BONEHAT.
SIGH
YES, SIRE.
OPEN IT!
CREEEEEAAAK
WHIRRR
CLICK-CLACK
BZZPTKRK
AW MAN I LEFT MY SANDWICH IN THE BREAK ROOM
DRIVE YOU FOOL DRIVE
NO YOU ARE NOT TURNING AROUND FOR A SANDWICH
NOOOOO

STORY Continues.

SHE IS WELL! MY DARLING, GORGEOUS DAUGHTER IS BACK!
HOW **ARE** YOU, MY DEAREST! YOU DON'T LOOK EMACIATED OR **ANYTHING!** DID THEY FEED YOU WELL?
AT ONE POINT I ATE A LITTLE GIRL TO KEEP HER QUIET.
CAPITAL! CAPITAL STRATEGY! MY DARLING GIRL IS HER FATHER'S OWN DAUGHTER!
I, **ALSO,** HAVE BEEN KNOWN TO **EAT** MY ENEMIES AT A MOMENT'S NOTICE!
IN FACT I HAVE MY CARVING-AX RIGHT HERE IF YOU'D LIKE TO SEE IT
I'M GOOD. **WOULD** LIKE TO USE A REGULAR BATHROOM SOMETIME SOON THOUGH.
Malki!

BUT WH-WHAT ABOUT THE —
THE **BOMB?** OH, THEREIN LIES A TALE OF **IDIOCY.**
YOUR **KIDNAPPERS,** LORD BONEHEAD, ARE **DEAD.**

"AFTER CONSUMING THE GIRL, I DECIDED TO **IMPERSONATE** HER AND ESCAPE.
"TO MY DISMAY, I DISCOVERED HOW **FAR** WE WERE FROM **ANYWHERE.**
"BUT THEN I FOUND A PAIR OF **MATTER-TRANSPORTERS** LYING UNUSED AND ABANDONED! THE KIDNAPPERS HAD BEEN USING THEM FOR **SPACE HEATERS.**"
IDIOTS DON'T KNOW WHAT THEY'VE **GOT** HERE!
THESE THINGS COST LIKE **TEN GRAND** AT BEST BUY!

"SOON I WAS DISCOVERED AND IMPRISONED – BUT WAS ABLE TO CONVINCE MY CAPTORS THAT I'D NEED ONE OF THE HEATERS TO STAY WARM, IF THEY DIDN'T WANT ME TO DIE OF CHILL.
I HAVE NO PROBLEM WITH YOU DYING OF CHILL.
B-BUT THE RANSOM! AND LORD BONE-HAT!
YOU ATE MY DAUGHTER!
THEN I KEPT ONE EAR POKED THROUGH THE TRANSPORTER...
AND THE INSTANT THE BOMB WAS TRIGGERED, TRADED PLACES WITH IT IN THE PIANO!
PERSONALLY I THOUGHT IT WAS VERY CLEVER.
OH, QUITE. SO, UH...I GUESS MAYBE I HAVE TO DO THIS THE TRADITIONAL WAY...
DEBORAH, WILL YOU MARRY ME?
HAH!
AFTER YOU HAD ME KIDNAPPED?
WHAT
"WHEN THEY HAD TROUBLE RIGGING THEIR BOMB, I WAS ABLE TO FURTHER CONVINCE THEM THAT THE DYNAMITE NEEDED TO BE HEATED...SO THEY PUT THE OTHER END OF THE TRANSPORTER INSIDE THE PIANO."
AWFUL NICE OF THE PRINCESS TO HELP US OUT WITH THIS.
WELL, YOU KNOW SOME PEOPLE. ALWAYS HAVE TO BE INVOLVED.
AAAAAHHHHHHH
OH GREAT KING – IN YOUR FIERCE WISDOM AND MERCY – MAY I ASK JUST ONE SMALL BOON IN THIS TERRIBLE HOUR OF RAGE –
PLEASE – I BEG OF YOU, MY LIEGE –
SAVE ME A DRUMSTICK
END!

MALADY MATRIX

What's all this

No doubt you have noticed the words along the edge of each left-hand page of this book. These are the 49 elements of the MALADY MATRIX. By combining them in various clever ways, we have discovered that from these humble elements flow the remedies to nearly all known afflictions.*

How it works

The four charts on the facing page ask questions of your condition, and assign numerical values to each answer. In this fashion every relevant facet of the condition is communicated to the system. Please be sure to answer honestly, to ensure maximum effectiveness. There is no need to be discreet with the matrix; we do not keep any records that can be subpoenaed later.

The four numerical values are assigned code letters: A, B, C, or E. (D was unavailable.) These correspond to pages in this book: the AB digits together are a page number, and the CE digits are likewise a second page number.

*Many afflictions are not yet known. It's always possible that you have one of those. After all, Lou Gehrig puzzled everybody. Perhaps you have Your Name's Disease.

The pages of the book are then juxtaposed in the manner detailed in the illustration above:

Step 1 Find the two 2-digit page numbers corresponding to your result from the matrix
Step 2 Align these pages as shown to assemble a directive from the component phrases
Step 3 (not shown) Enact the directive

The process is simple and delightful. Let us give an example.

What general type of malady is this? You are plagued with nosebleeds after a psychic visitation, so you choose 'Physical.' **A: 0**

How severe is the malady? It is persistent despite your best efforts with tape. **B: 4**

What is the cause? Although this would seem to be a trauma, you provoked the visitation with hubris. **C: 8**

What is your overall level of health? A comics fan, you are chronically sickly. **E: 2**

Thus, you would turn to pages 4 and 82.

What general type of malady is this?

Physical – An affliction of the body, incl. muscles, blood, organs, humours	0
Mental – A problem of cognition, incl. memory loss, disorientation, stupidity	1
Disorder – Hearing voices, hallucinations, insomnia, hysteria, *et cetera*	2
Existential – Complaints of the middle class, such as ennui, insecurity, anxiety	3
Other – Gender confusion, cute overload, megalomania, hiccups, *et cetera*	4

A ▢

How severe is the malady?

Mild – A mere annoyance now and again, niggling or infrequent	0
Moderate – Stiff upper lip, tolerable for the worst of it, but a bit of a bother	2
Constant – Distractions are a welcome relief, mathematics prove difficult	4
Severe – Pharmaceutical budget has become a source of tension in the family	6
Unbearable – Impossible to even focus on this page, such is the unending agony	8

B ▢

What is the cause?

Trauma – A distinct event in the past has specifically caused this circumstance	5
Congenital – This has been preordained in one's genetic code; there is no escape	6
Environmental – Contaminants, toxins, everything the news warned us about	7
Indulgence – No self-control at all; OR, simply the trappings of success	8
Imaginary – Affliction resides purely in the realm of the theoretical. Buck up then	9

C ▢

What is your overall level of health?

Miserable – Constantly racked with countless ailments; this is just the latest	0
Troubled – Prone to accidents and sickness, really do *not* need this right now	2
Coping – Used to taking this sort of thing in stride; after all, we're merely meatbags	4
Decent – Ocasionally fall under the weather, but normally manage just fine	6
Healthy – Save for this problem, the picture of vigor. Nothing can stop me	8

Exception: We have no data for CE pair 9-8. If your problem is imaginary and you are perfectly healthy, you are fine. For further details please consult our companion volume, *Problems You Probably Don't Have (But Might).* $89.95 + SHIPPING

E

unicorn foam

TROUBLESHOOTING

I am not sure what exactly is wrong with me

   WebMD and other on-line sources may be of assistance to help you refine a cluttered collection of symptoms into a precise diagnosis. When in doubt, always bias amateur diagnoses towards the more severe—better that treatment is overkill, rather than not effective enough.

I do not know how best to describe my malady

   The matrix on the previous page is only useful if you are able to clearly break your problem into its component characteristics. However, if multiple options each seem appropriate for your particular problem, you may run the matrix for each possible permutation and simply average the resultant directives.

I have more than one problem

   You may run the matrix for each problem or symptom separately, and then enact all the resultant directives. The entire concert should be performed continually until each of the initial symptoms have vanished.

Performing a matrix directive has birthed some new problem

   Simply run the matrix for the new problem. You may continue in this fashion for as long as necessary without ill effect.

My specific problem is not addressed

   Have you considered the possibility that something is on backwards? *(See diagram)*

Possible cause of any problems outside the scope of this book

INDEX.

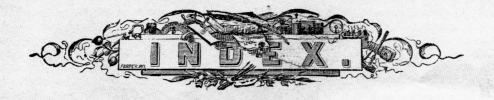

Index of Last Lines

AUTHOR’S NOTE

Thus draws to its end another book that is nominally about something else, but which is really about comic-strips. (Let's be honest.) If I were a crass marketer, I would tell you to rush immediately to your local Internets amd write an Amazon review of this book. But what would such a request mean? It would mean that I cared more about SELLING BOOKS than about seizing this final opportunity to make a personal connection with *you,* the reader for whom the entire endeavor has been conceived.

And surely this is not the case! For have I not, just three sentences previous, been *brutally honest* with you in a way that only the dearest of friends can be? This is a book of comics! It is not an actual medical manual, despite the many times in the prior pages when I have insisted that it is. Those were lies! They were meant to provoke chuckles and a warm sense of recognition, as in, "Ooh, Cousin Marty would *really* get a kick out of this book." And he *would,* wouldn't he? It's *just the thing* for Cousin Marty! Cousin Marty is *my kind of guy!*

But this frankness leads us to a sort of stalemate. I have lied to you for ninety-four pages, and then been honest with you for one. (This one.) How can I expect you to believe me *now?*

I know. I shall issue two versions of this book. If you are the type of person whom I adore and whose health and well-being are wonderfully valuable to me, I shall ensure that your copy of the book has a painting of Steamovak on the next page. If you are an oaf for whom I care little, there shall be nothing.

Once again, I thank you humbly for the gift of your attention. I shall keep it with my favorite treasures.

MALKI !08!

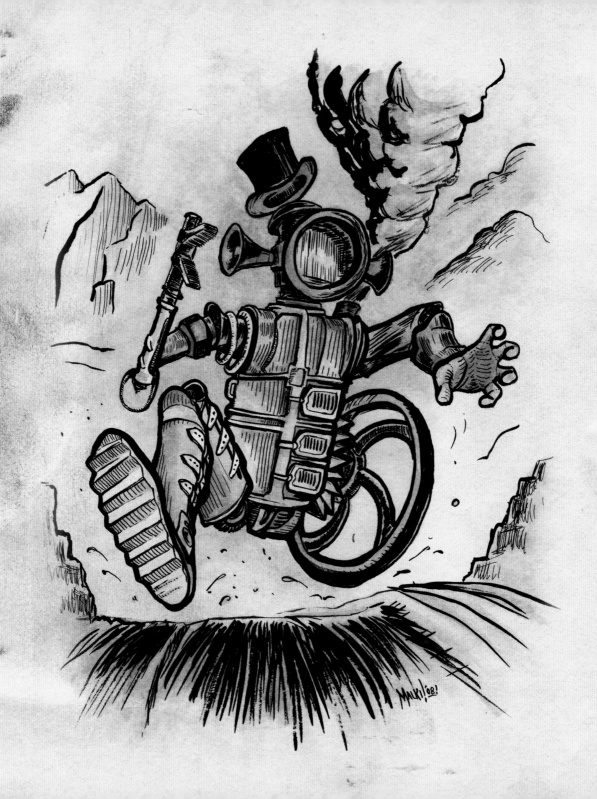

The Wondermark Series
By David Malki !

MR. MALKI'S style is very much like that of the discerning citizen's favorite author, the late lamented Percy Whitesnatch, Jr., but his tales are thoroughly up-to-date. The stories are as sharp as they are clever, and will prove of absorbing interest to hardy folks everywhere.

Bindings vary. All volumes illustrated. Some feature color; others eschew the practice. Price per volume on par with market rates. Available from your local bookseller or via WONDERMARK.COM.

The Annotated Wondermark
This, the very Earliest of all comic-strip collections, anthologizes the utter beginnings of the phenomenon in a portable container totalling some 88 pages of delight.

Beards of our Forefathers
A further collection of comic-strips—hard-bound in the manner of the book you now hold, and similar to it in many other respects as well. The recipient of many Lauds and much fervent Acclaim.

Clever Tricks to Stave Off Death
The latest strip-collection. You probably have seen this one already, somehow; our wager is that you are familiar enough with its contents that we may skip the explanation.

Dispatches from Wondermark Manor
A Parody Victorian Novel in three volumes, told not in Comics but rather in Prose, in a style aping the most absurd masters of Yester-Yore. Those who fancy this love it most dearly.

Earl the Elephant-Man Goes to Town
Unfortunately does not exist.

WONDERMARK ENTERPRISES;
DARK HORSE BOOKS;   } Publishers.